AMAZING DOT-TO-DOT PUZZLES

Conceptis Puzzles

PUZZLE
WRIGHT
PRESS

New York

PUZZLE WRIGHT PRESS

New York

An Imprint of Sterling Publishing
387 Park Avenue South
New York, NY 10016

ISBN 978-1-4549-1196-8

Distributed in Canada by Sterling Publishing
C/o Canadian Manda Group, 165 Dufferin Street
Toronto, Ontario, Canada M6K 3H6
Distributed in the United Kingdom by GMC Distribution Services
Castle Place, 166 High Street, Lewes, East Sussex, England BN7 1XU
Distributed in Australia by Capricorn Link (Australia) Pty. Ltd.
P.O. Box 704, Windsor, NSW 2756, Australia

For information about custom editions, special sales, and premium and corporate purchases,
please contact Sterling Special Sales at 800-805-5489 or specialsales@sterlingpublishing.com.

Manufactured in China

4 6 8 10 9 7 5

www.puzzlewright.com

•••••••••••••••••••• **Contents** ••••••••••••••••••

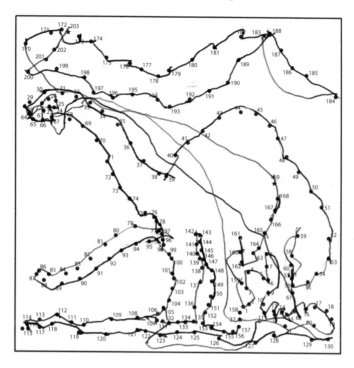

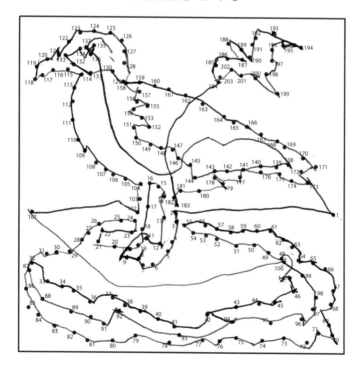

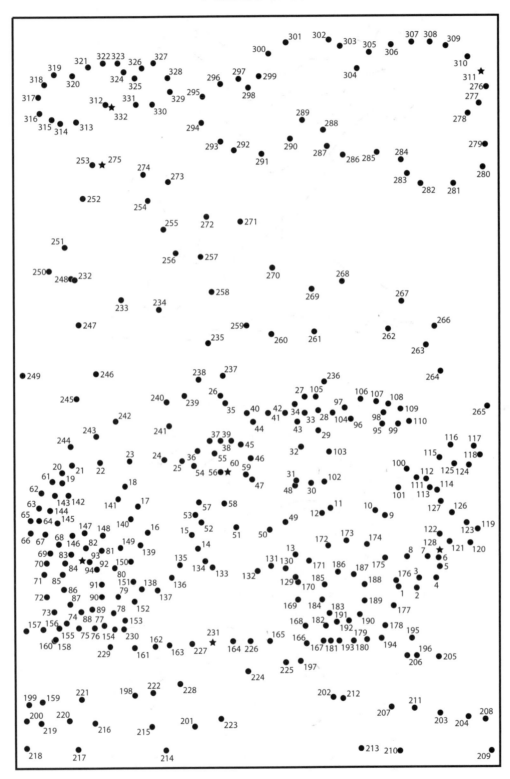

ANSWER, PAGE 81

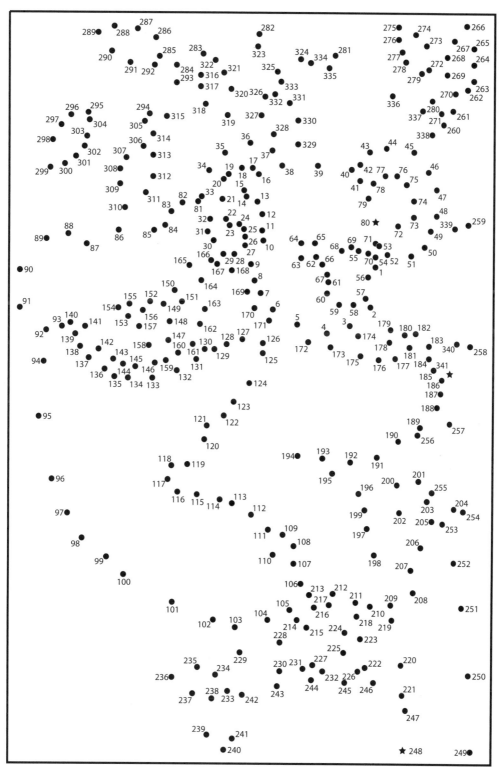

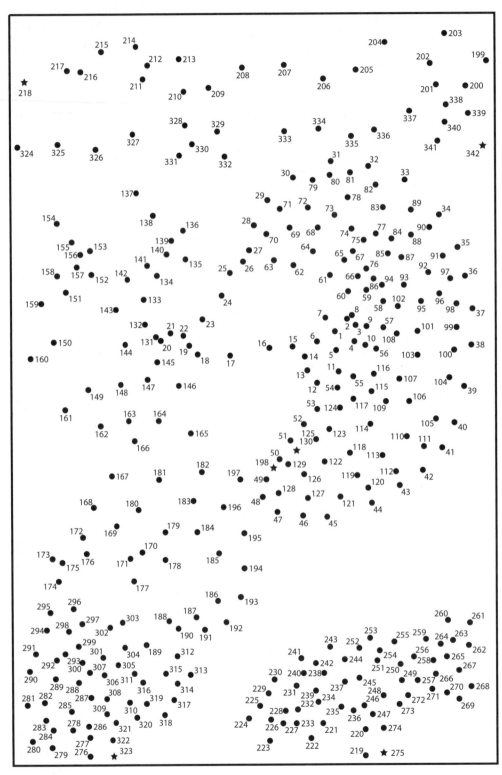

ANSWER, PAGE 81

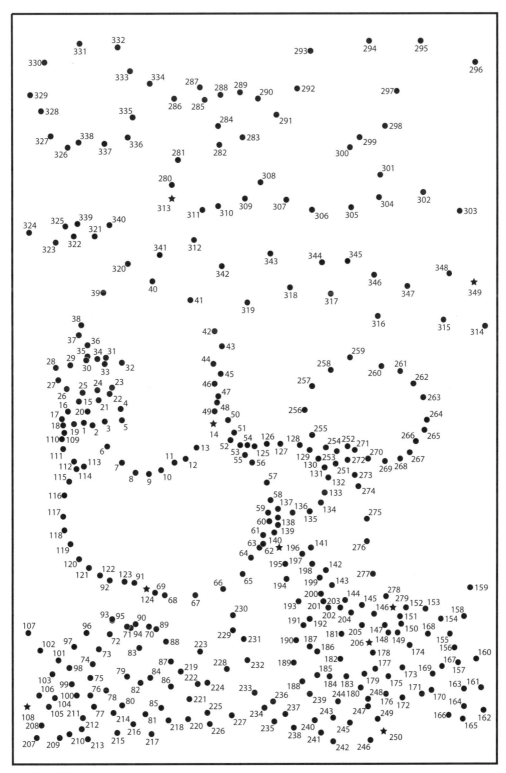

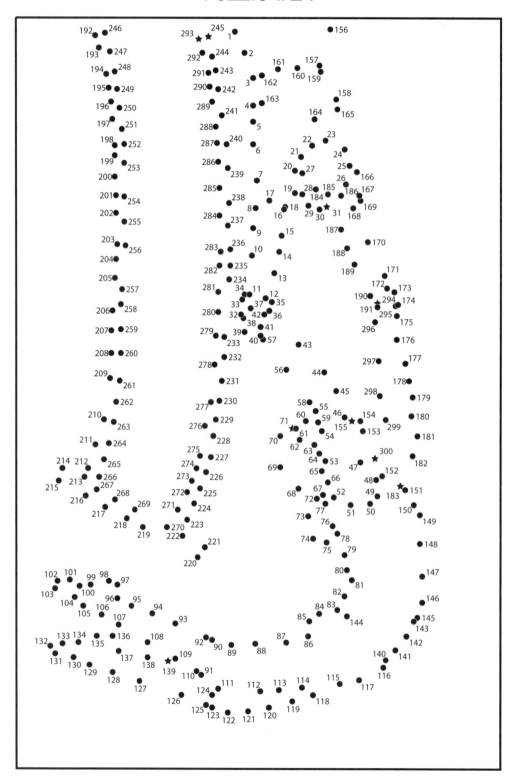

ANSWER, PAGE 82

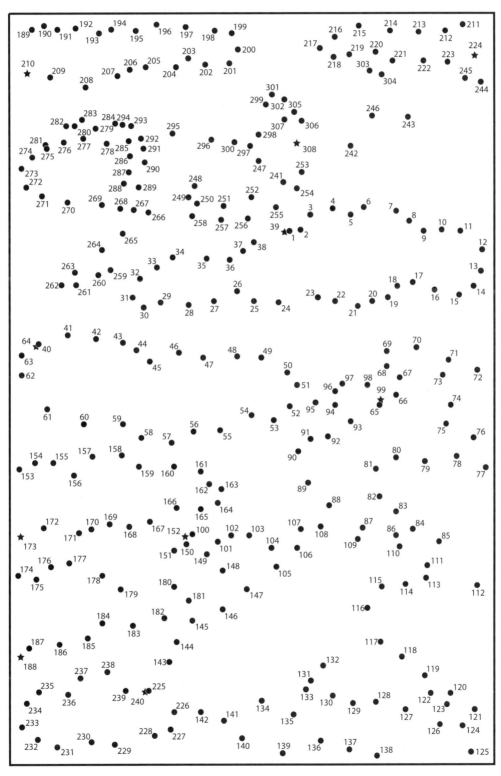

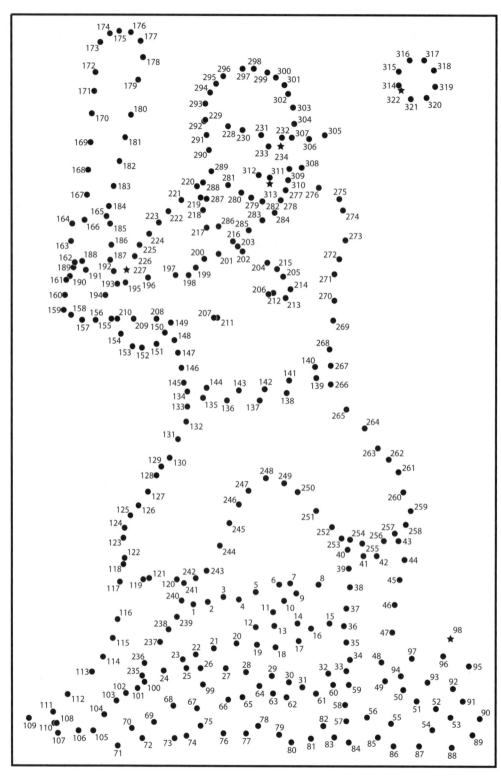

ANSWER, PAGE 82

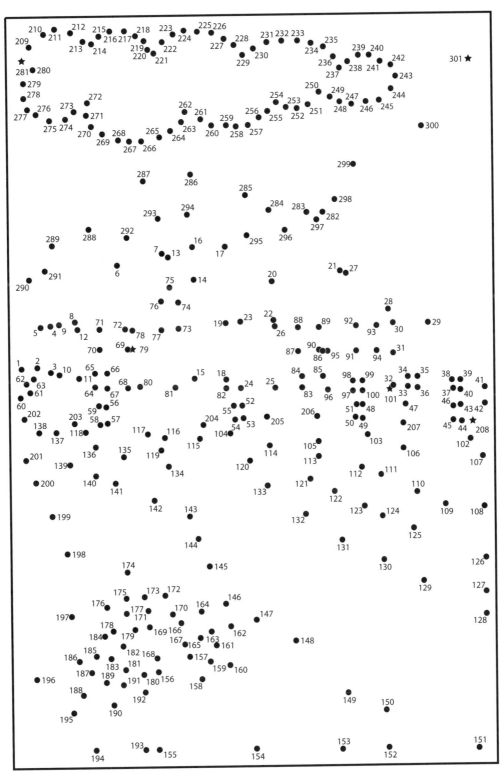

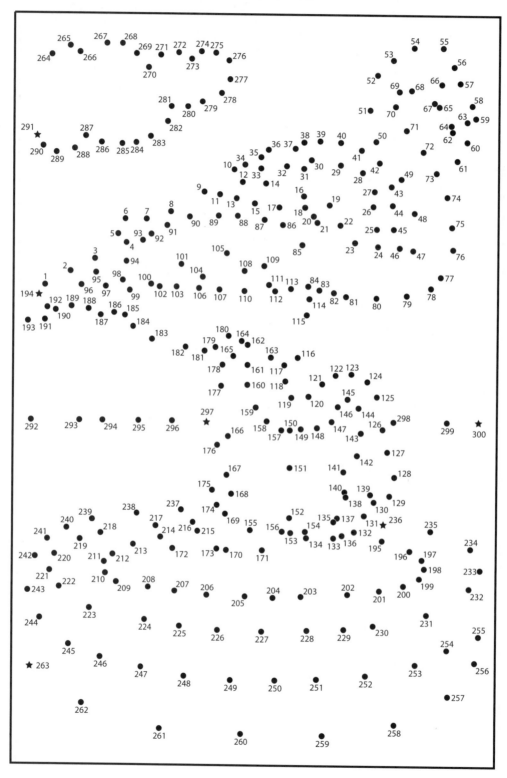

ANSWER, PAGE 83

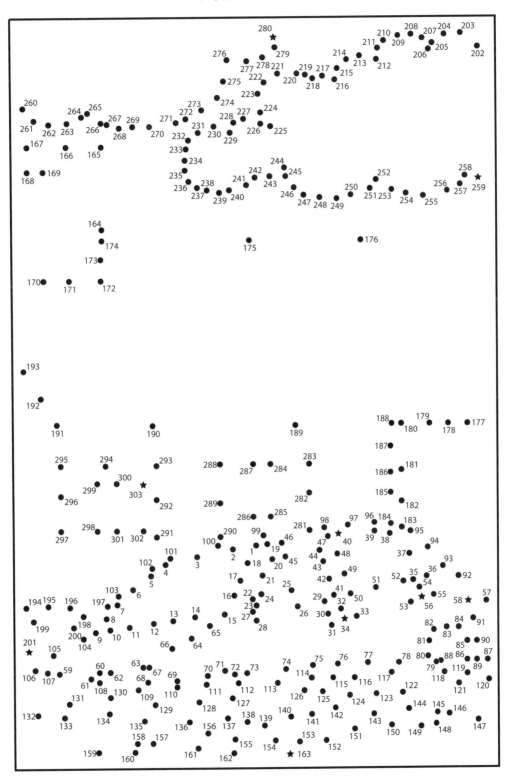

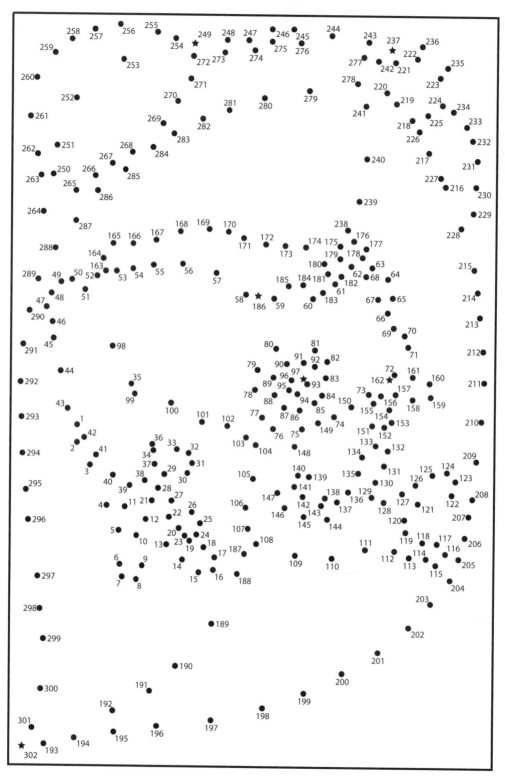

ANSWER, PAGE 83

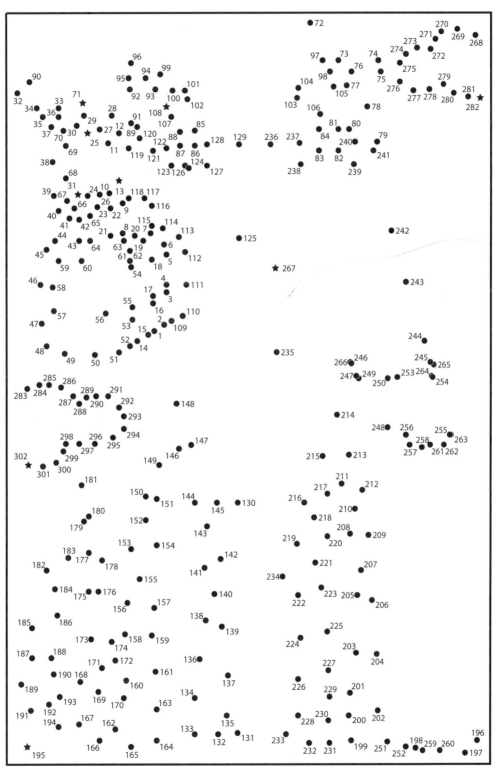

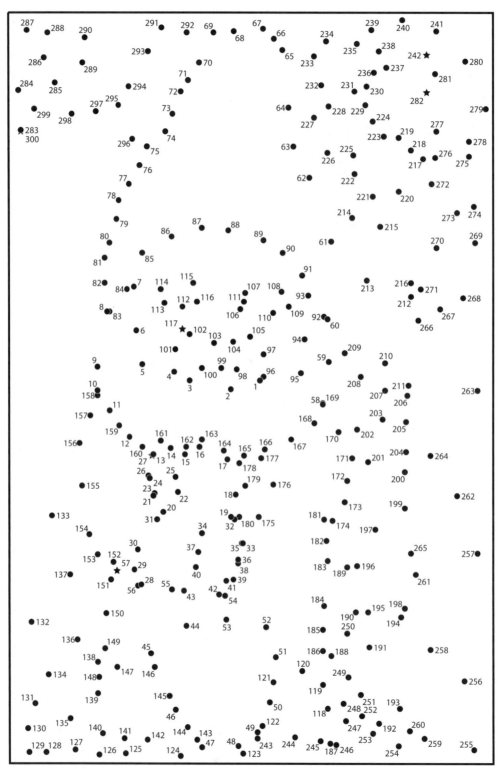

ANSWER, PAGE 84

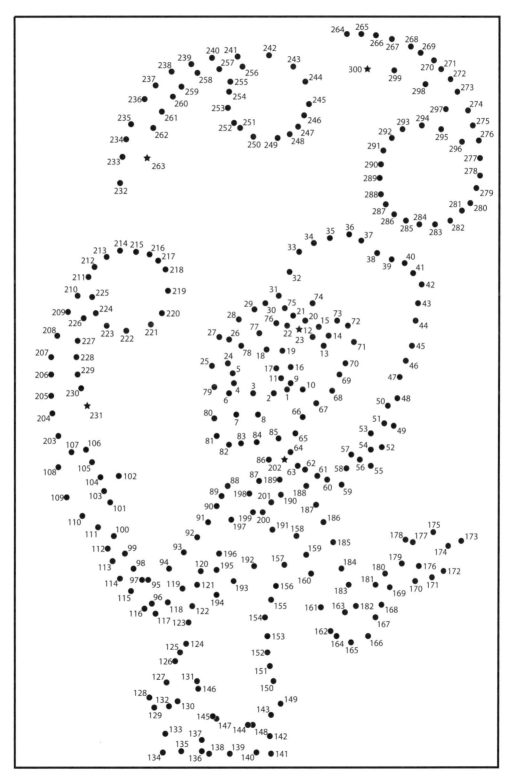

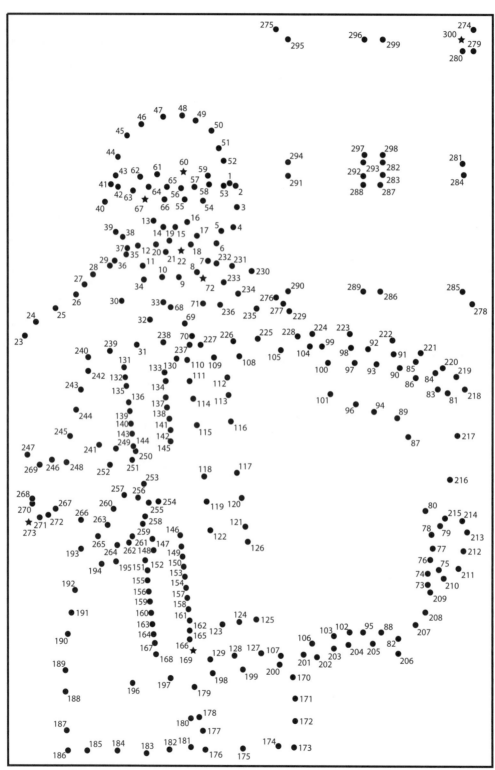

ANSWER, PAGE 84

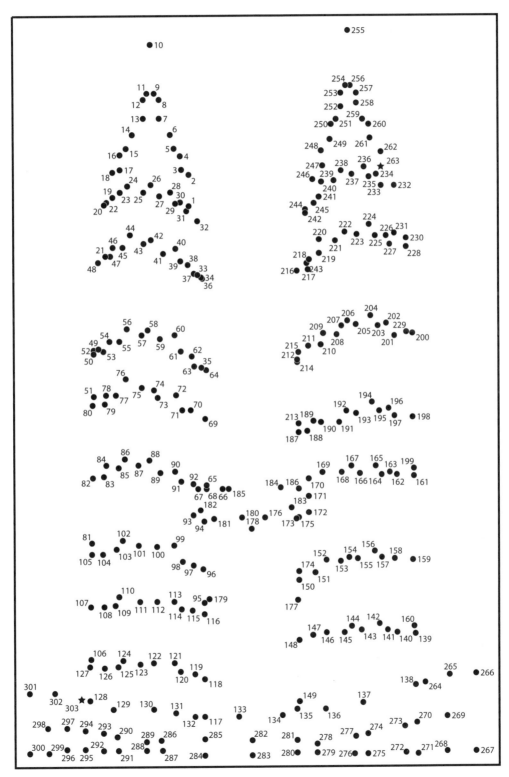

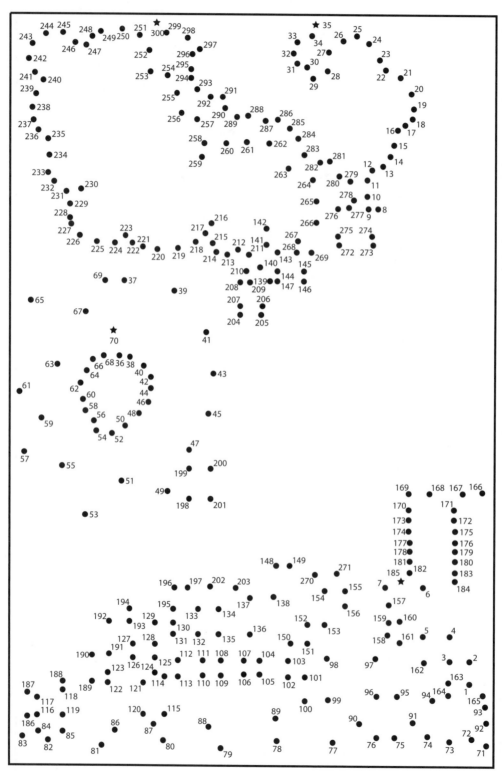

ANSWER, PAGE 85

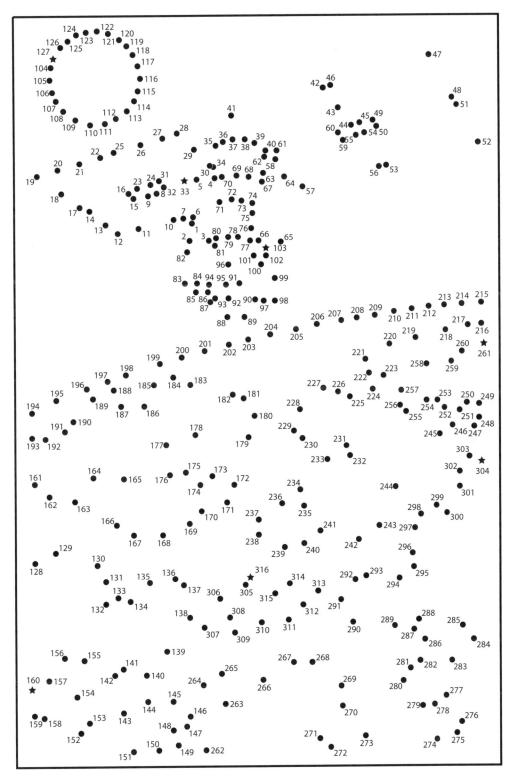

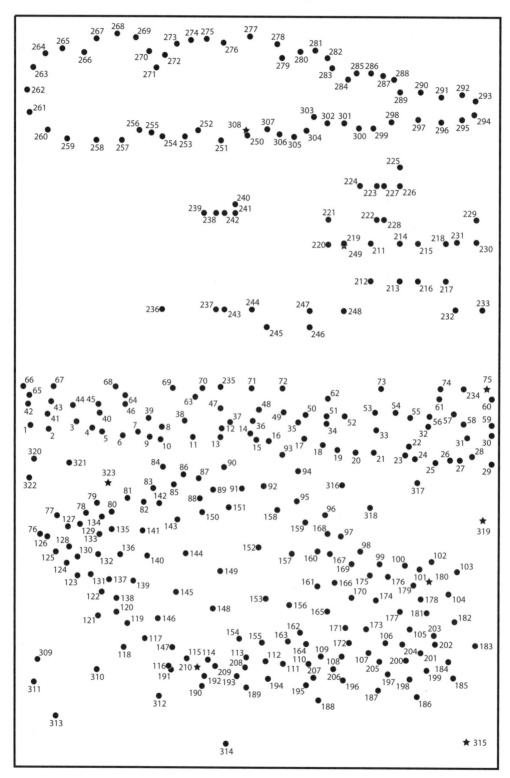

ANSWER, PAGE 85

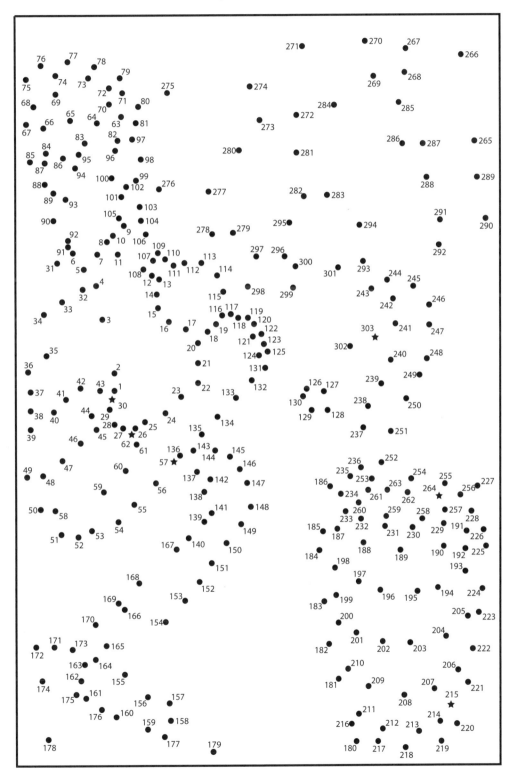

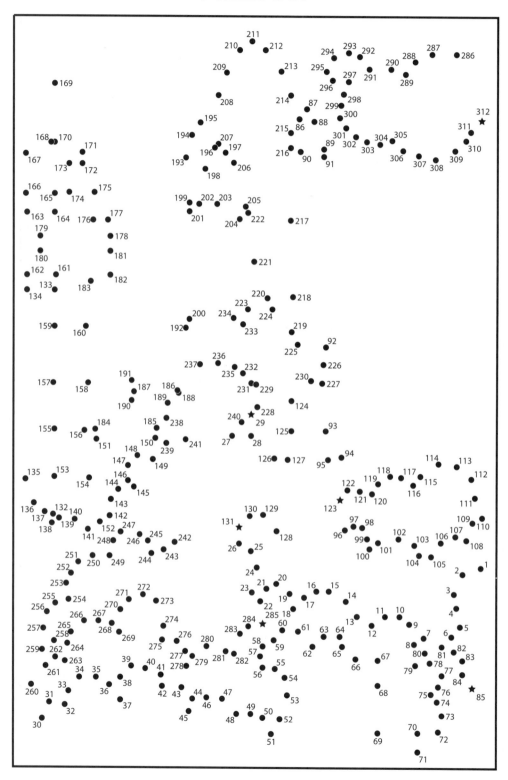

ANSWER, PAGE 86

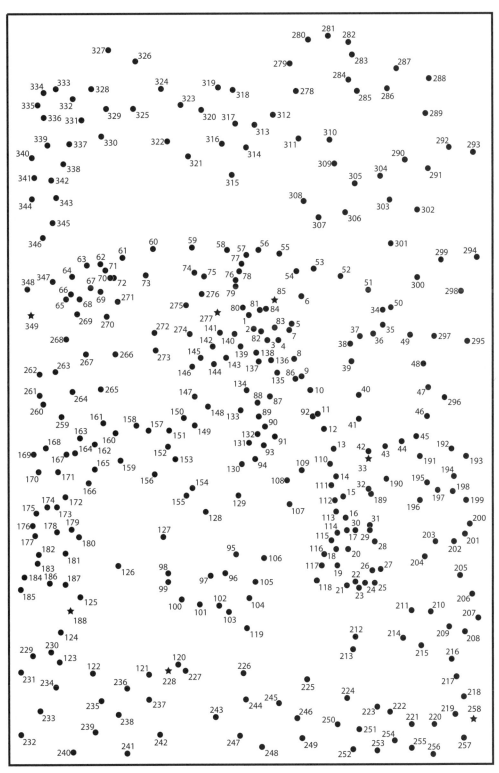

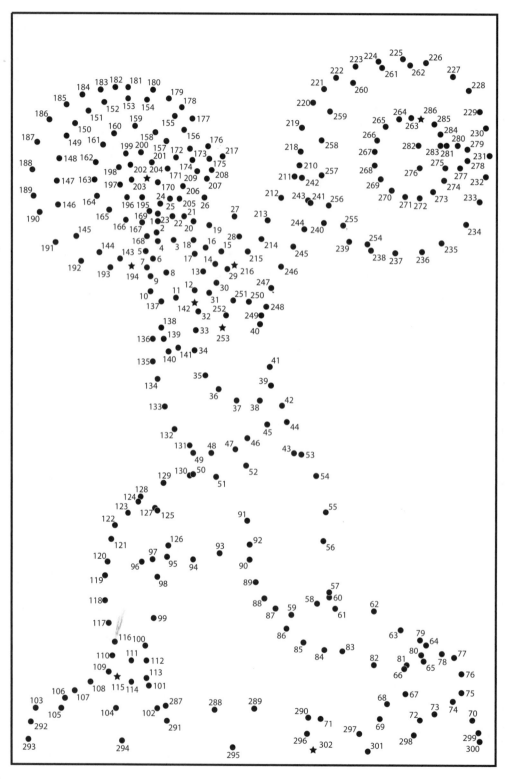

ANSWER, PAGE 86

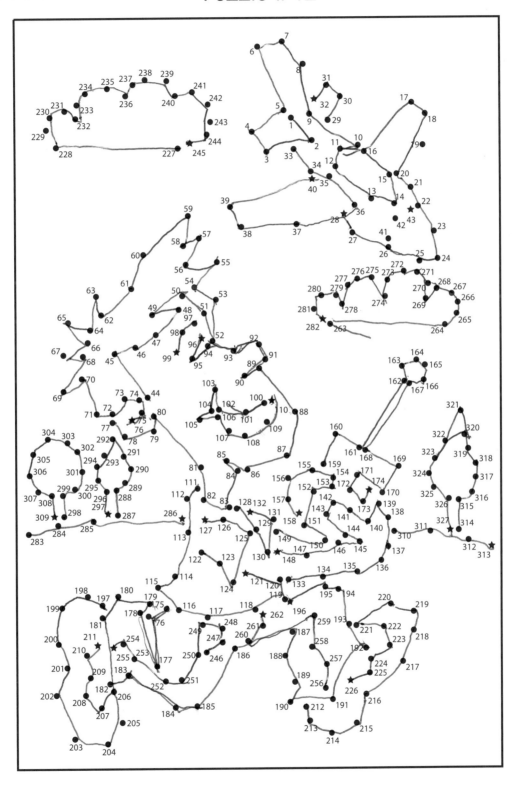

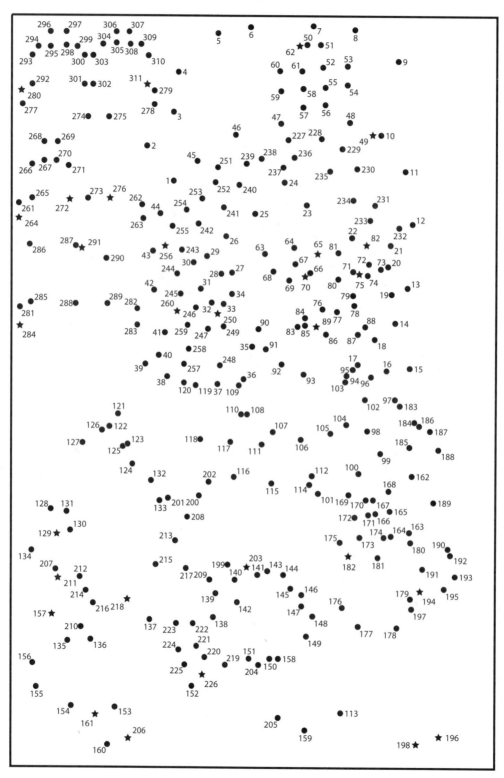

ANSWER, PAGE 87

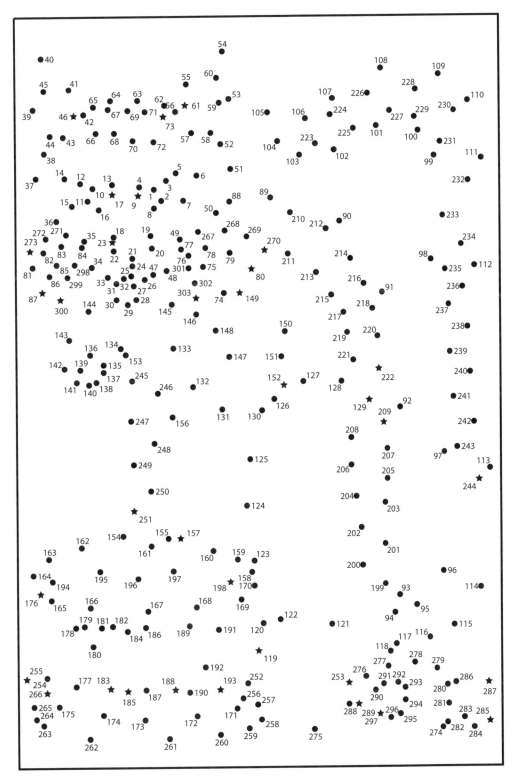

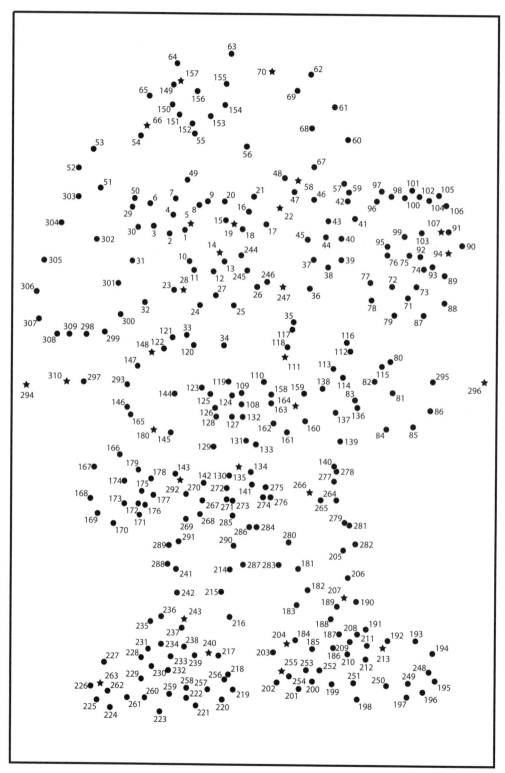

ANSWER, PAGE 88

Puzzle #46

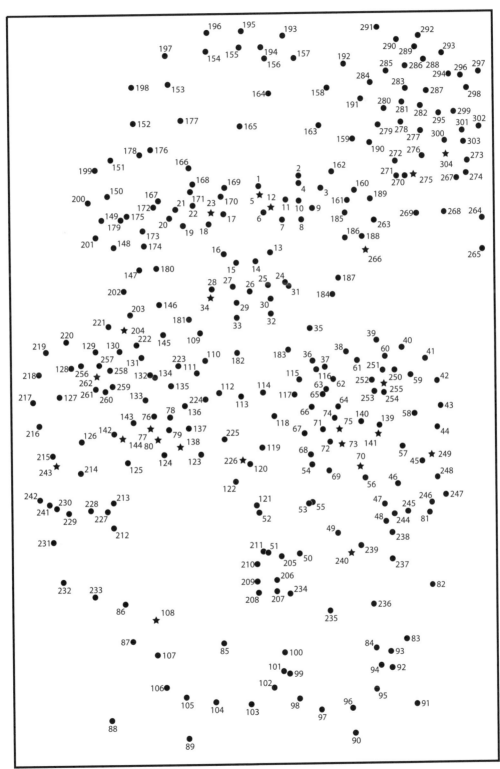

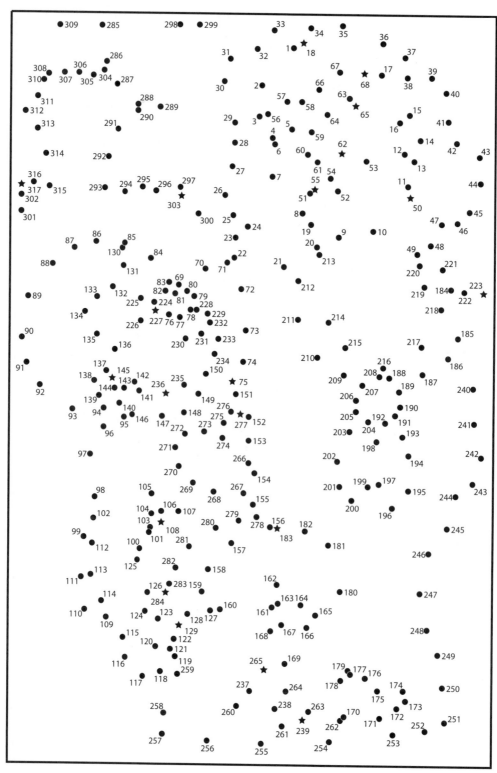

ANSWER, PAGE 88

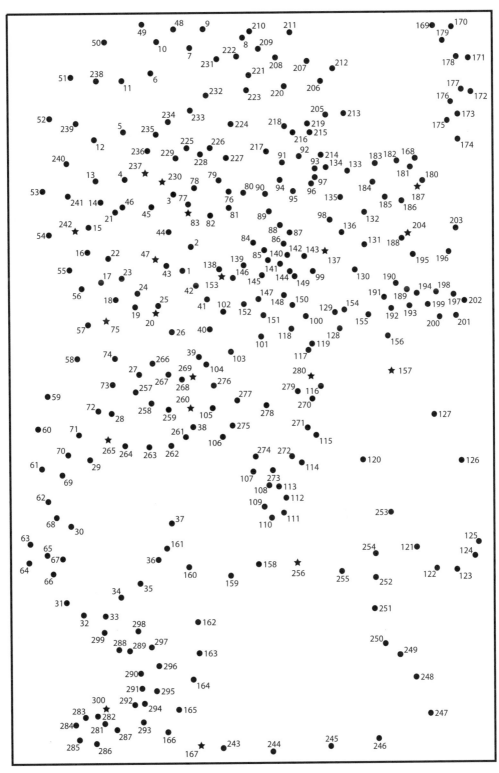

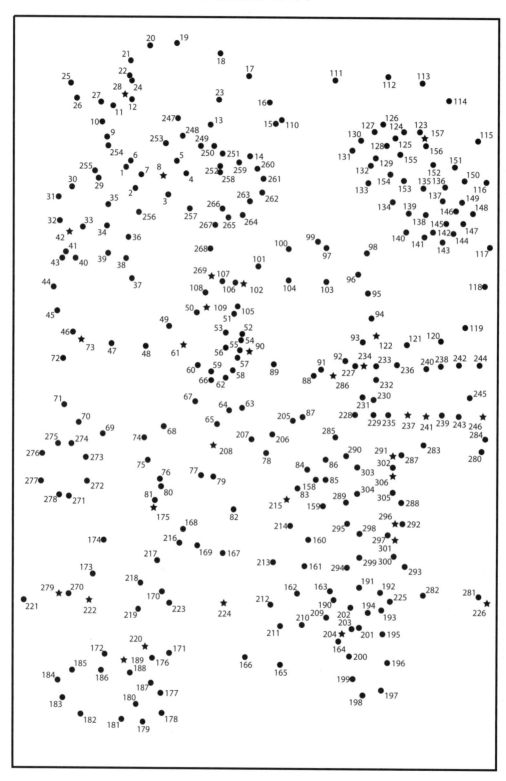

ANSWER, PAGE 89

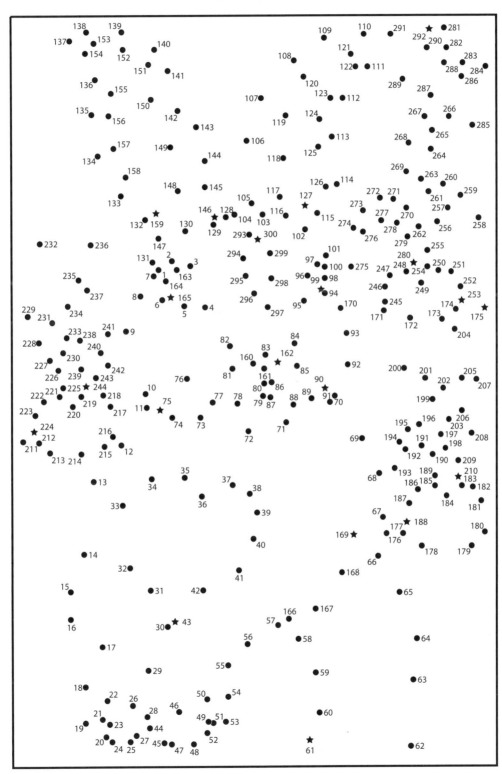

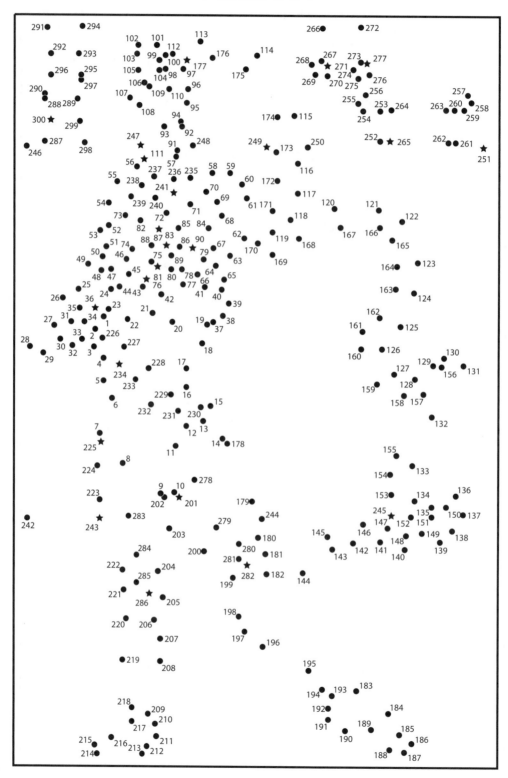

ANSWER, PAGE 89

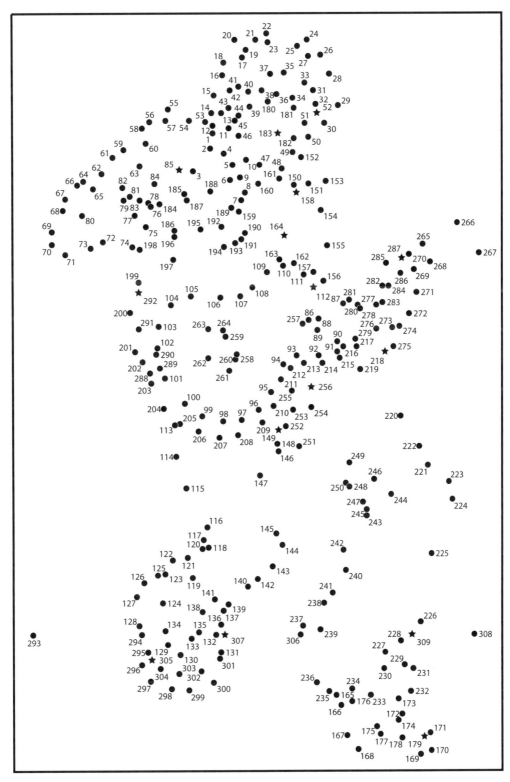

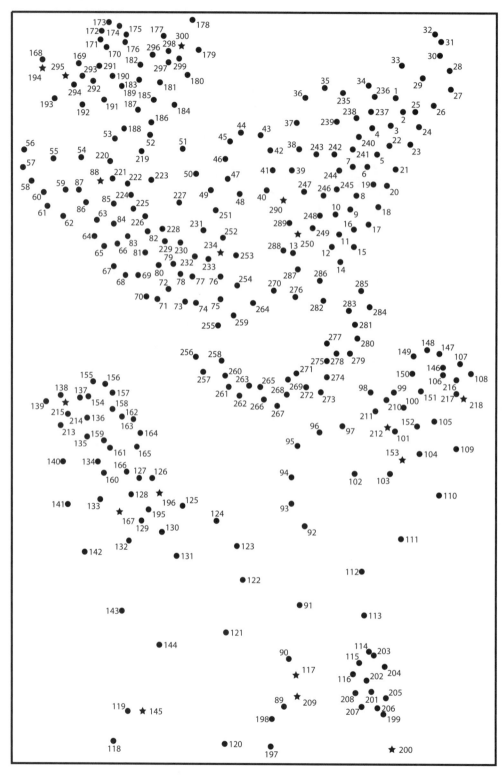

ANSWER, PAGE 90

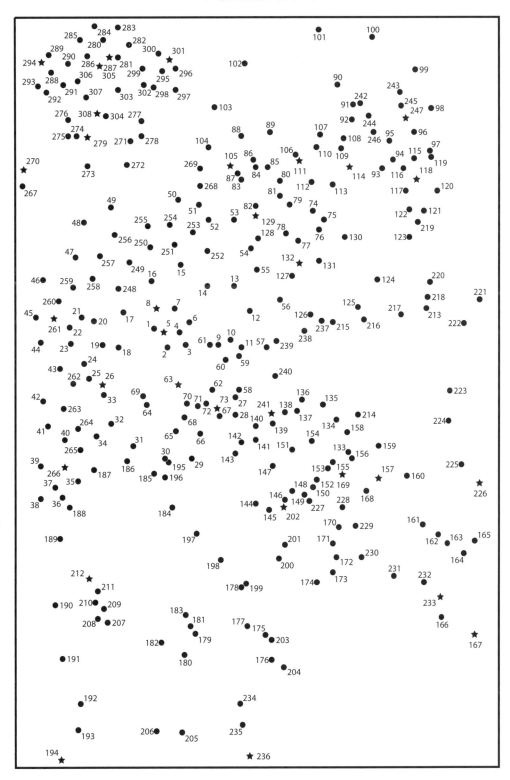

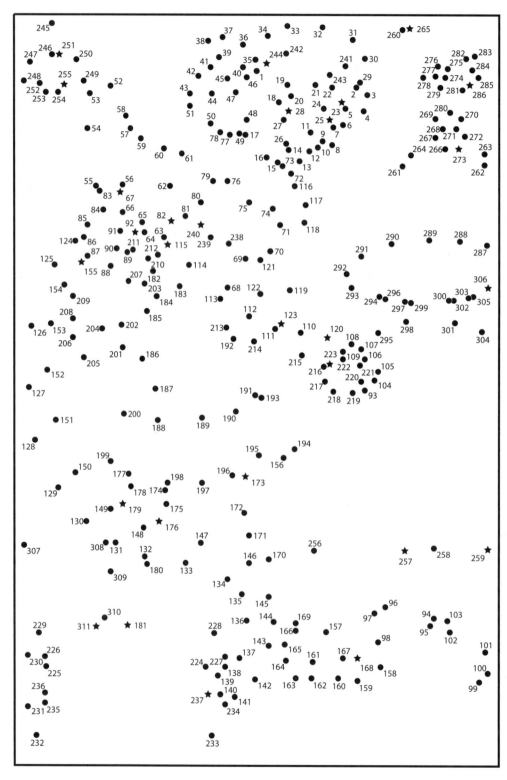

ANSWER, PAGE 90

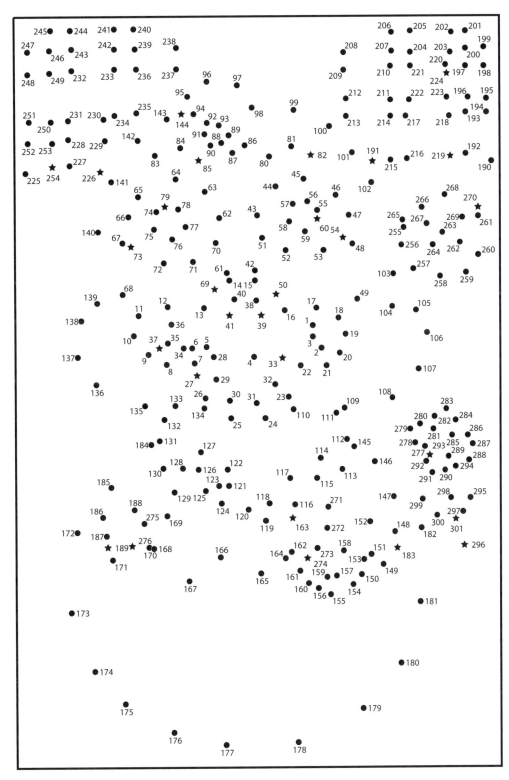

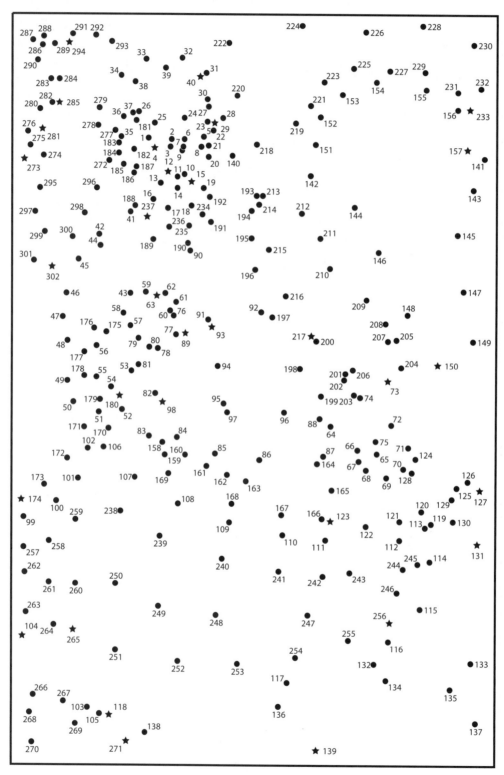

ANSWER, PAGE 91

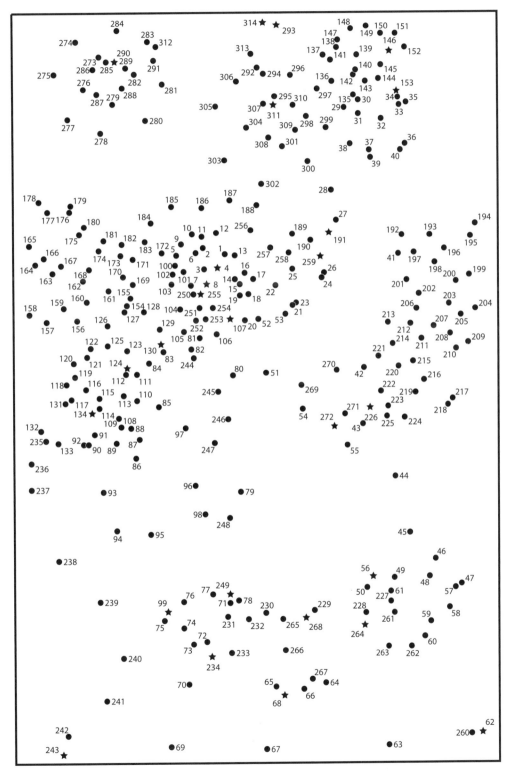

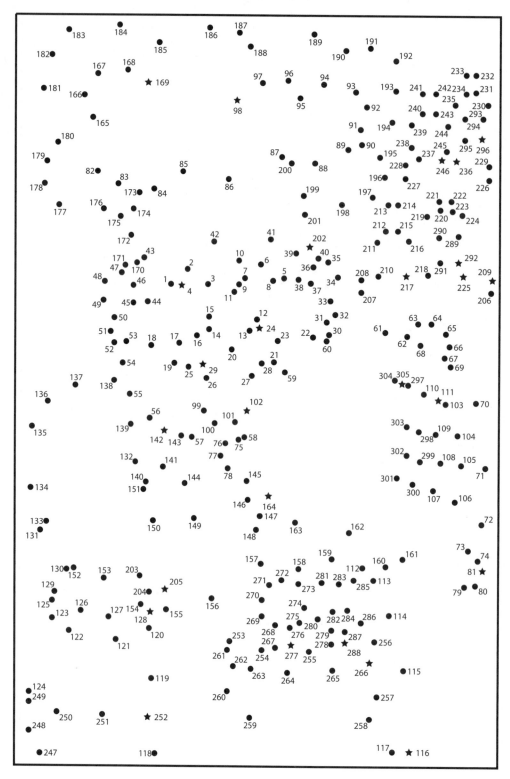

ANSWER, PAGE 91

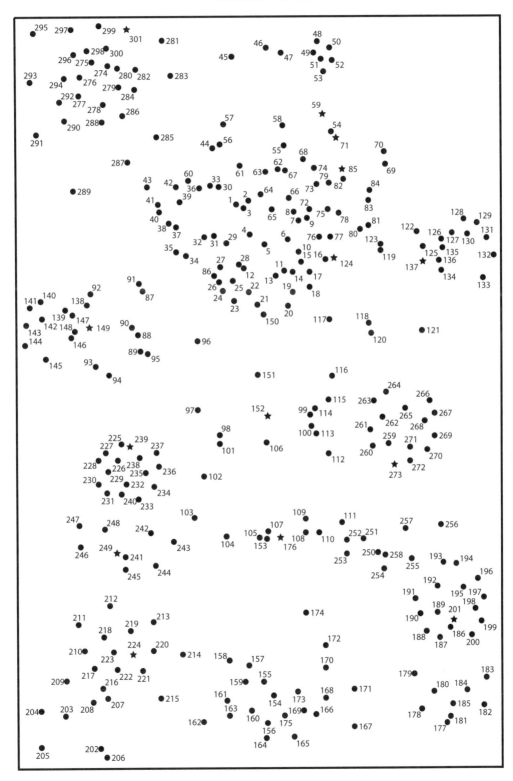

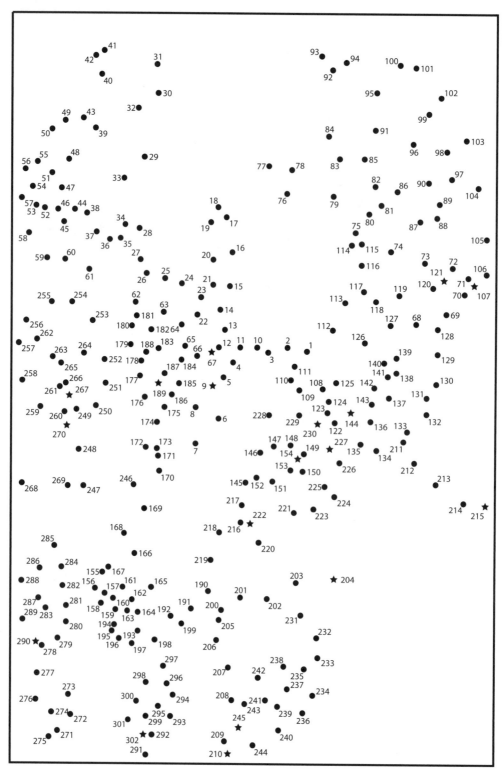

ANSWER, PAGE 92

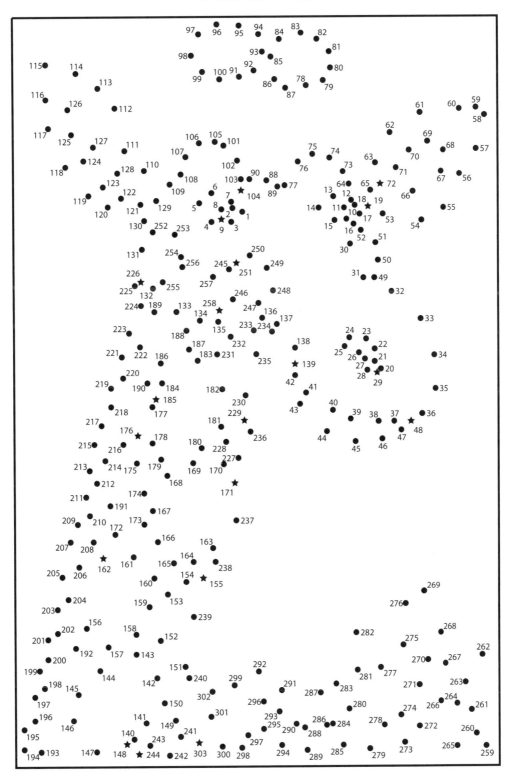

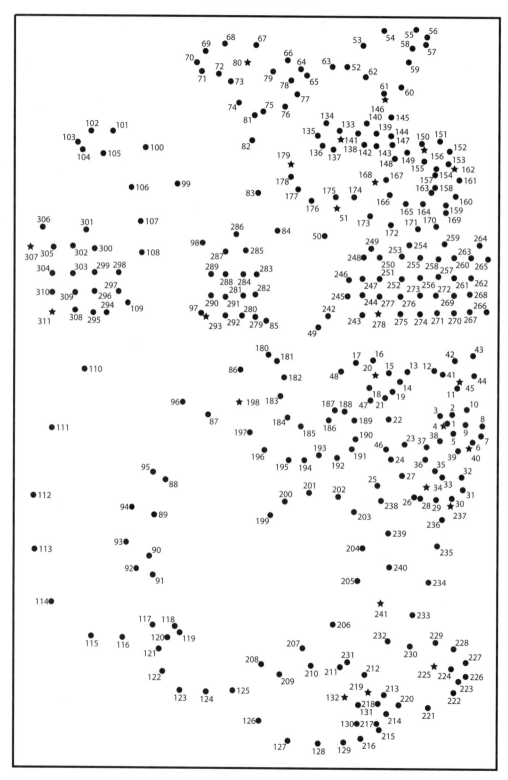

ANSWER, PAGE 92

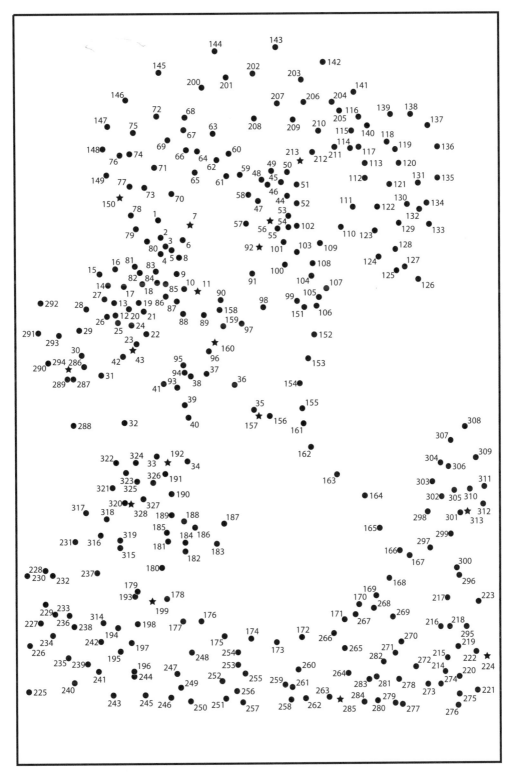

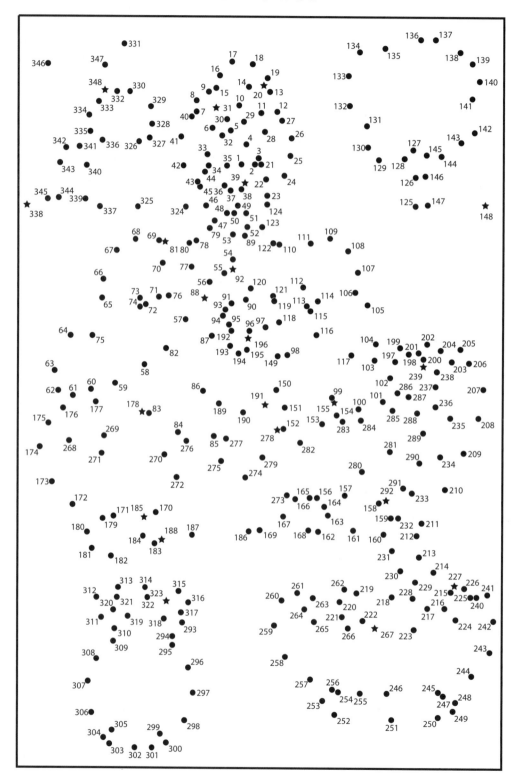

ANSWER, PAGE 93

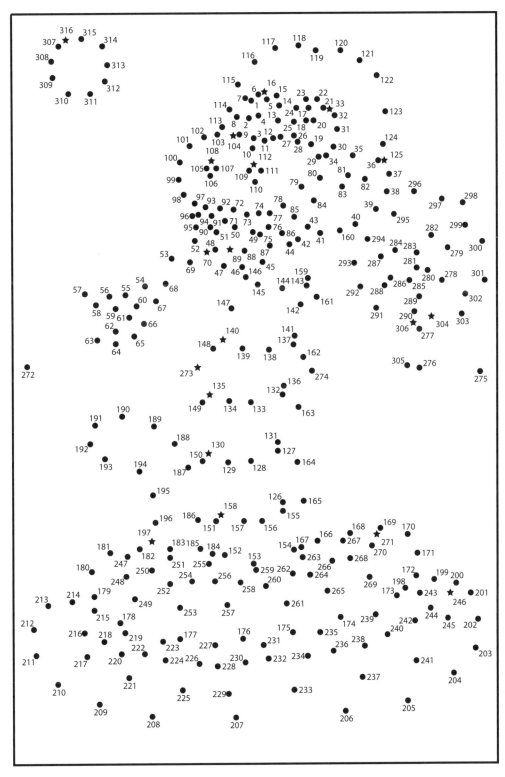

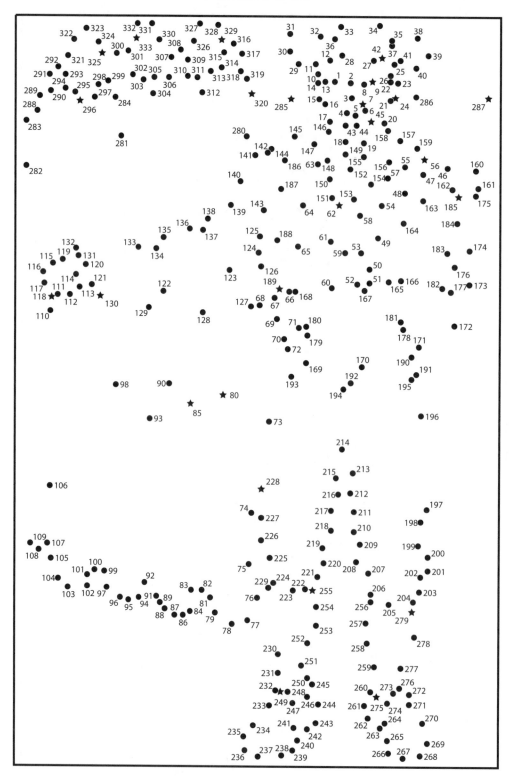

ANSWER, PAGE 93

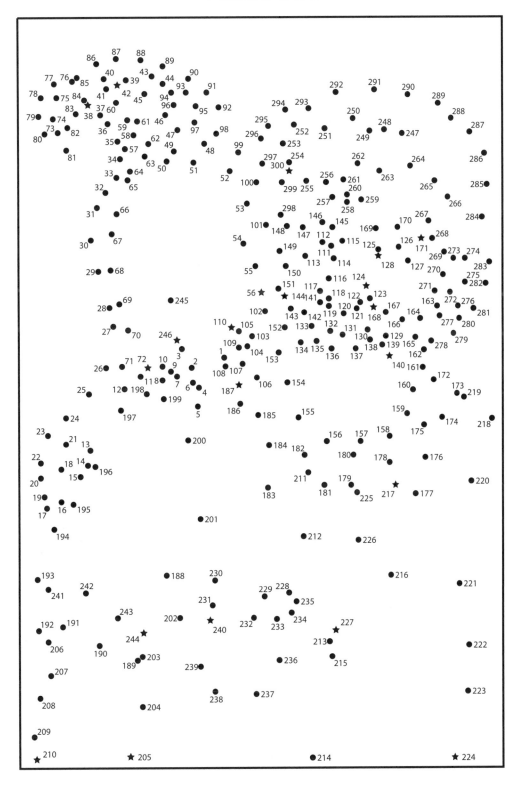

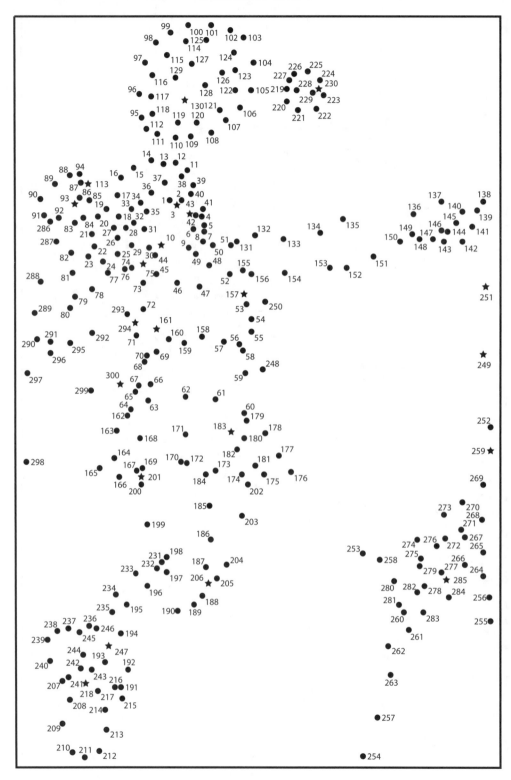

ANSWER, PAGE 94

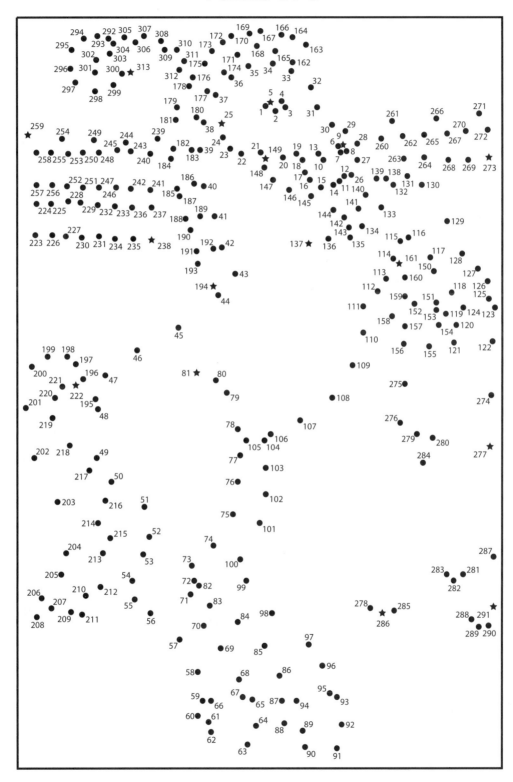

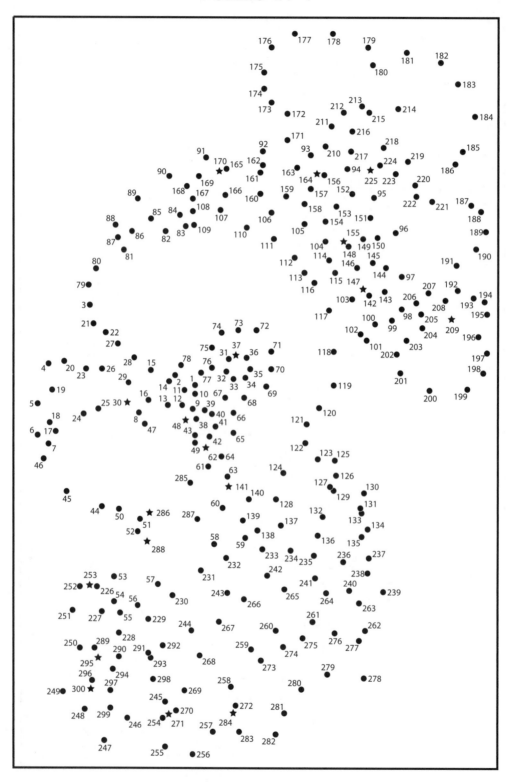

ANSWER, PAGE 94

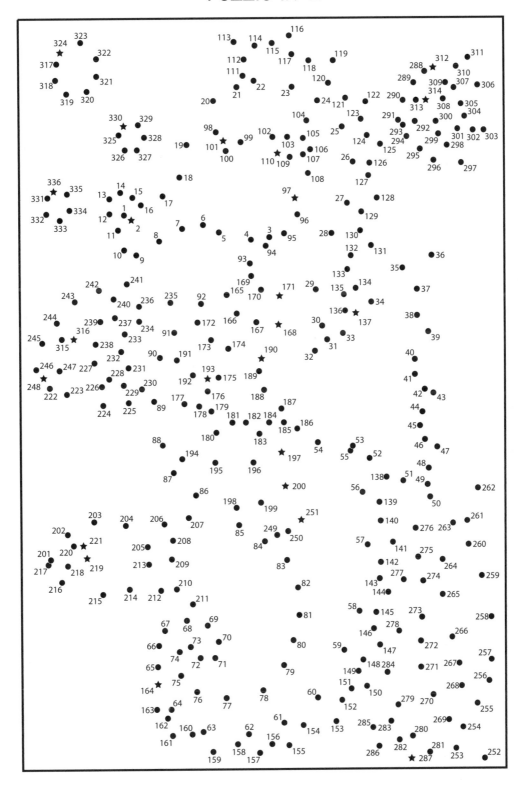

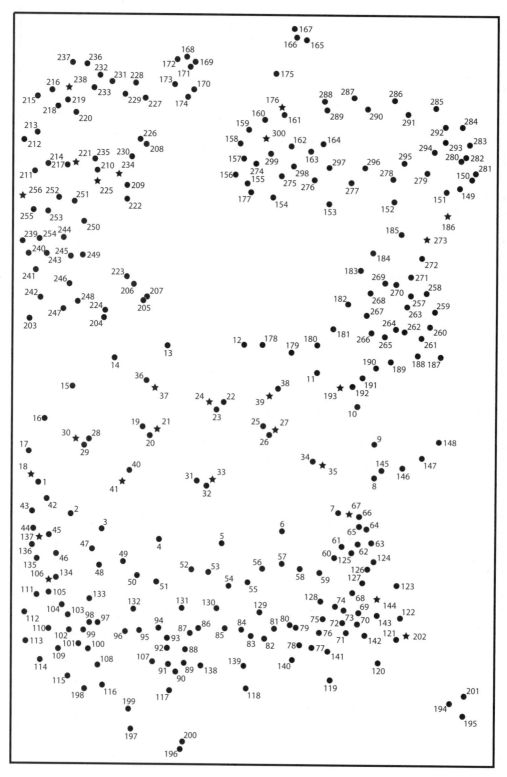

ANSWER, PAGE 95

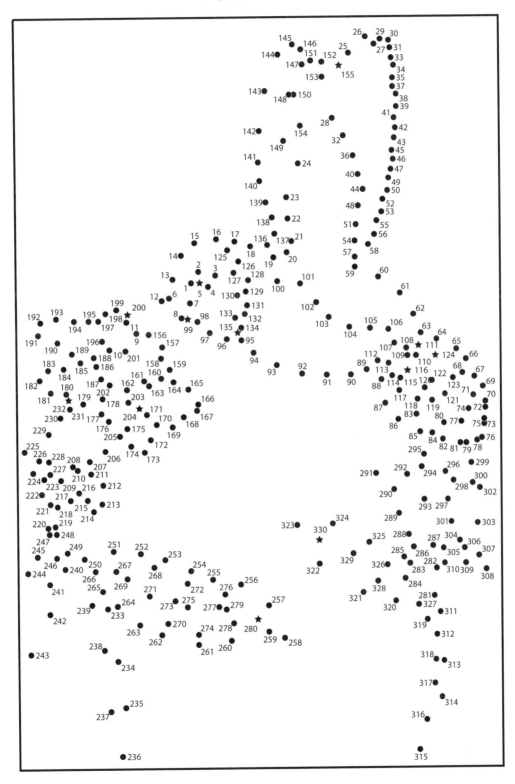

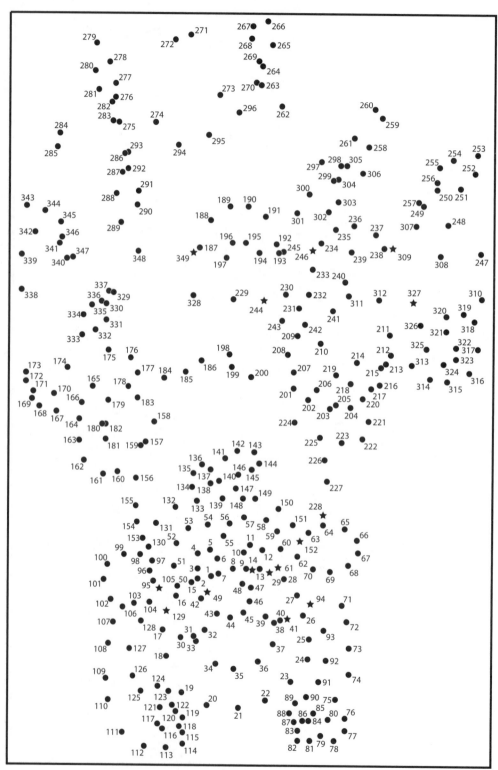

ANSWER, PAGE 95

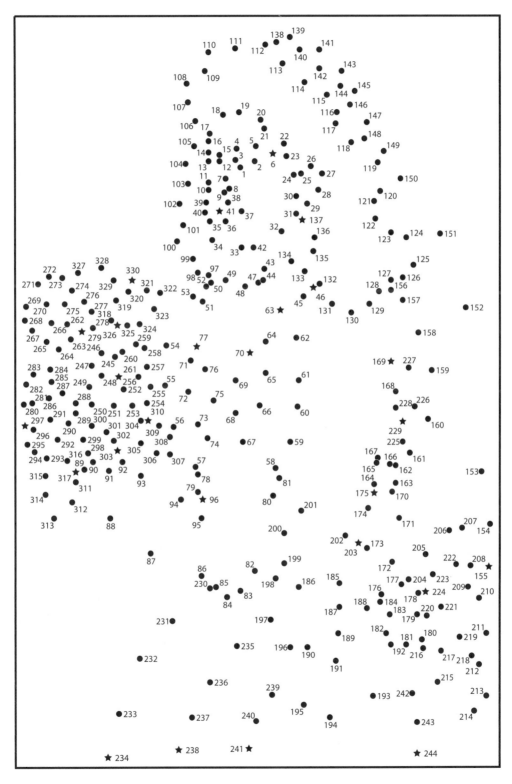

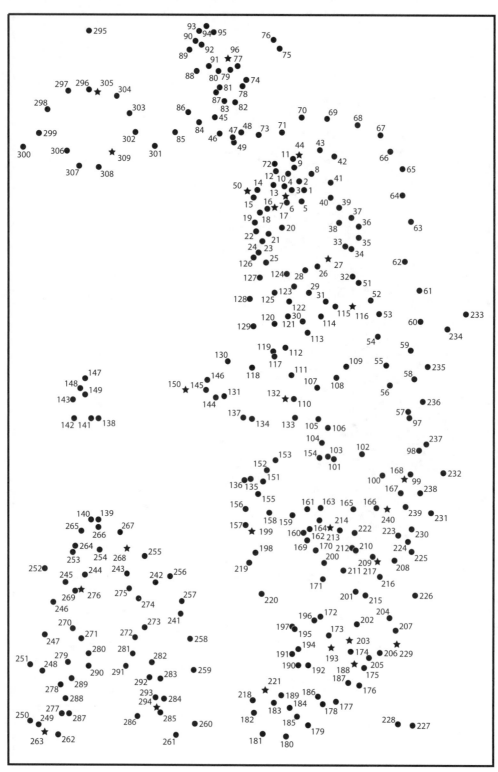

ANSWER, PAGE 96

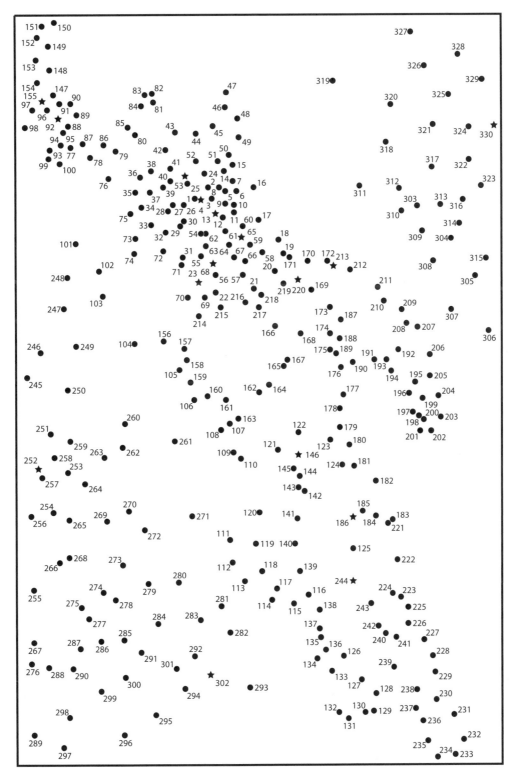

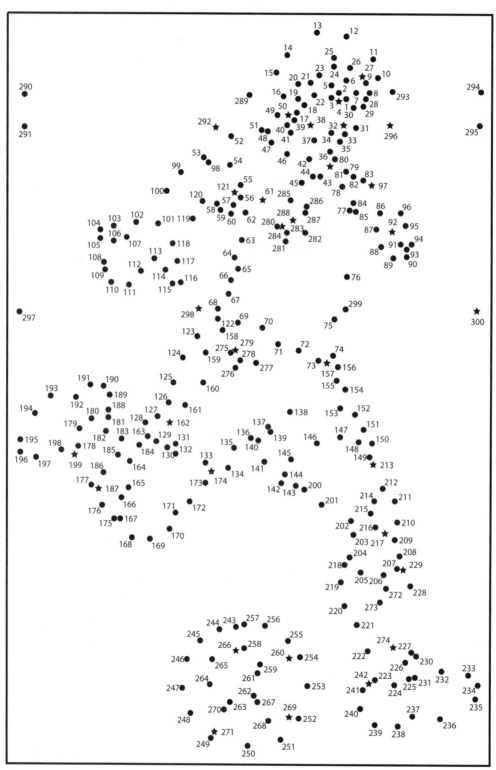

ANSWER, PAGE 96

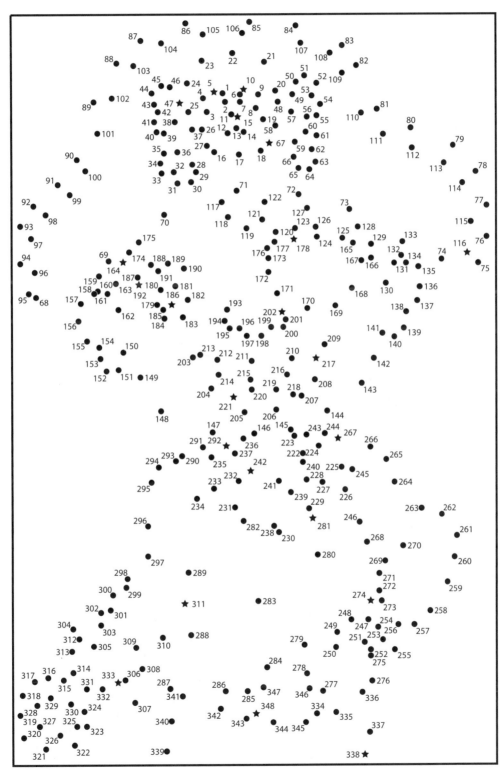

Puzzle #1

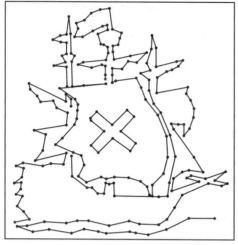

Puzzle #2

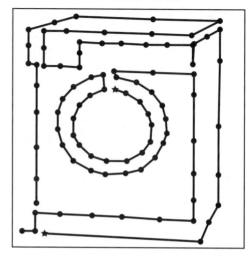

Puzzle #3

Puzzle #4

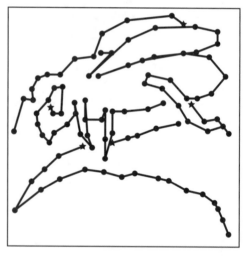

Puzzle #5

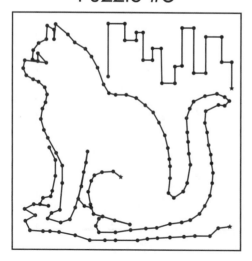

Puzzle #6

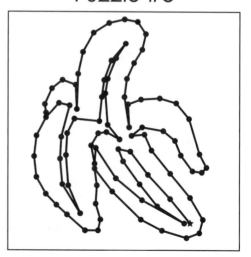

Puzzle #7

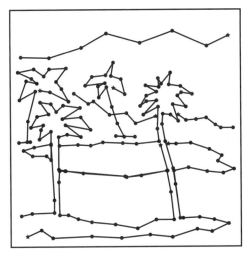

Puzzle #8

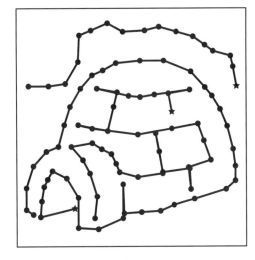

Puzzle #9

Puzzle #10

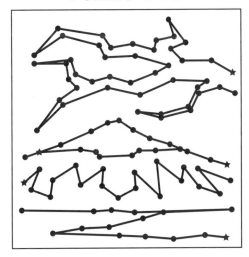

Puzzle #11

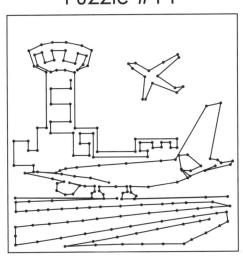

Puzzle #12

Puzzle #13

Puzzle #14

Puzzle #15

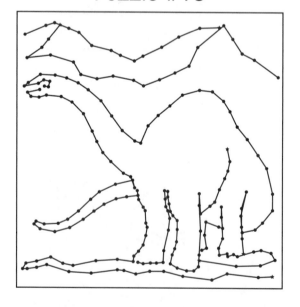

Puzzle #16

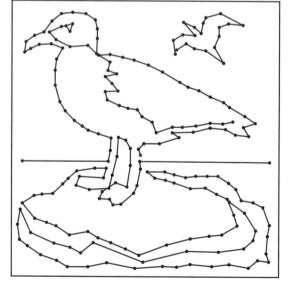

Puzzle #17

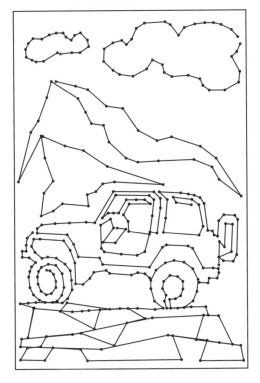

Puzzle #18

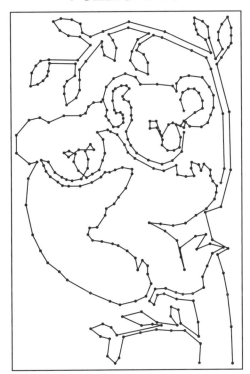

Puzzle #19

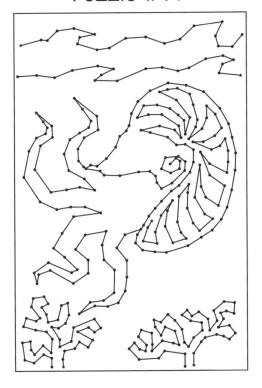

Puzzle #20

Puzzle #21

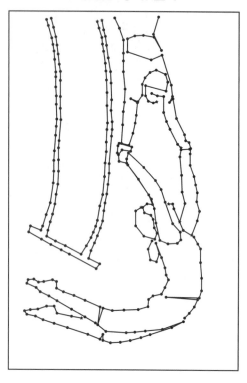

Puzzle #22

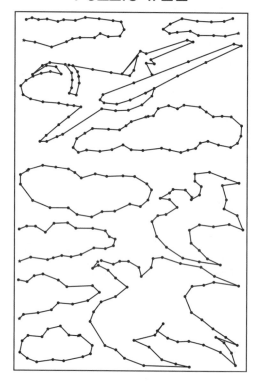

Puzzle #23

Puzzle #24

Puzzle #25

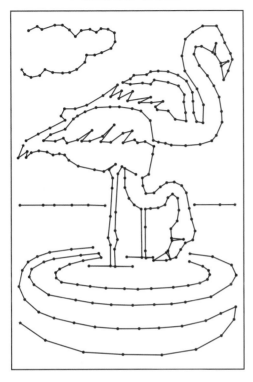

Puzzle #26

Puzzle #27

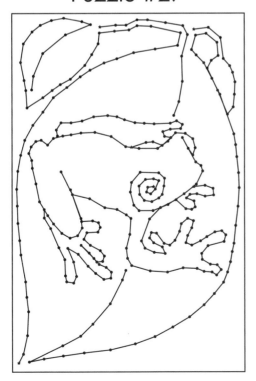

Puzzle #28

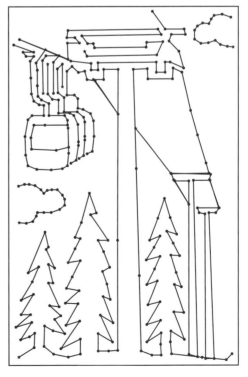

Puzzle #29

Puzzle #30

Puzzle #31

Puzzle #32

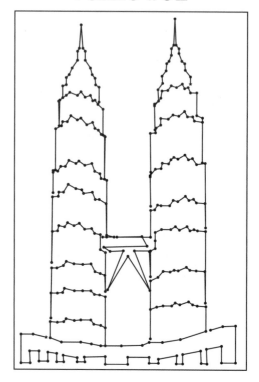

Puzzle #33

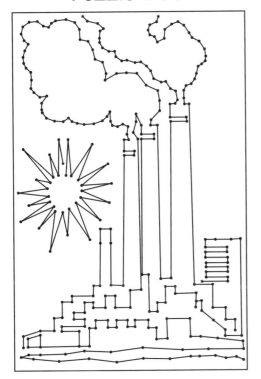

Puzzle #34

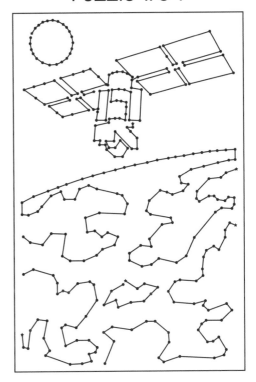

Puzzle #35

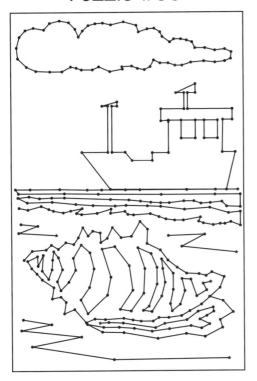

Puzzle #36

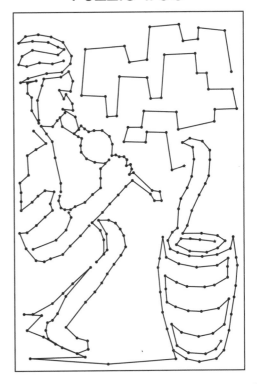

Puzzle #37

Puzzle #38

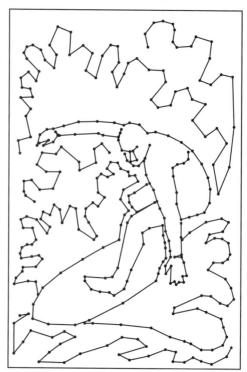

Puzzle #39

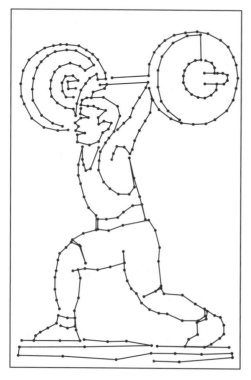

Puzzle #40

Puzzle #41

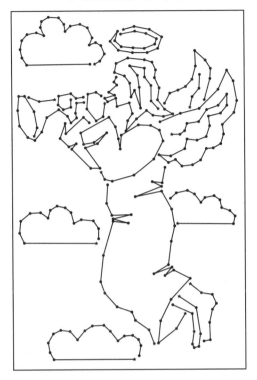

Puzzle #42

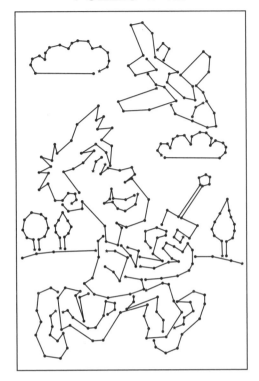

Puzzle #43

Puzzle #44

Puzzle #45

Puzzle #46

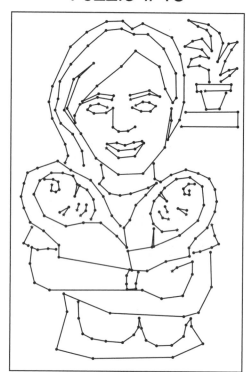

Puzzle #47

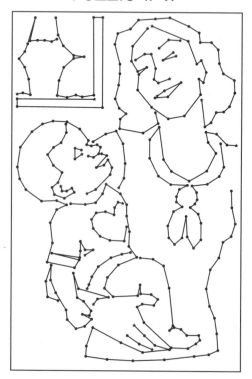

Puzzle #48

Puzzle #49

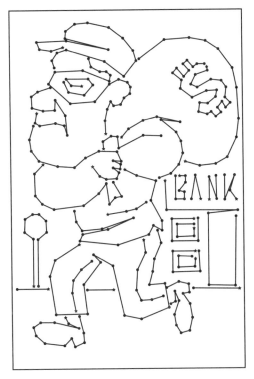

Puzzle #50

Puzzle #51

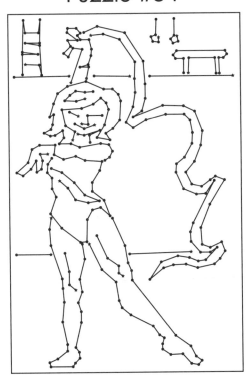

Puzzle #52

Puzzle #53

Puzzle #54

Puzzle #55

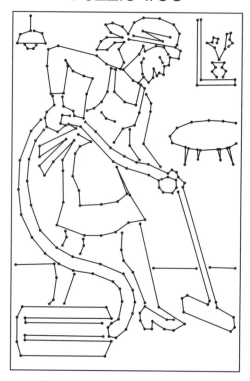

Puzzle #56

Puzzle #57

Puzzle #58

Puzzle #59

Puzzle #60

91

Puzzle #61

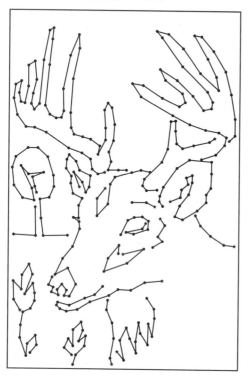

Puzzle #62

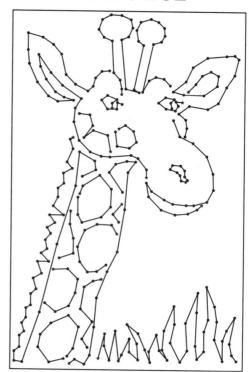

Puzzle #63

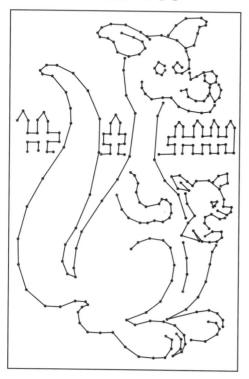

Puzzle #64

Puzzle #65

Puzzle #66

Puzzle #67

Puzzle #68

Puzzle #69

Puzzle #70

Puzzle #71

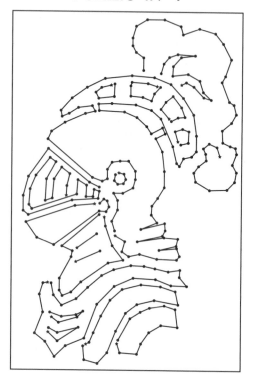

Puzzle #72

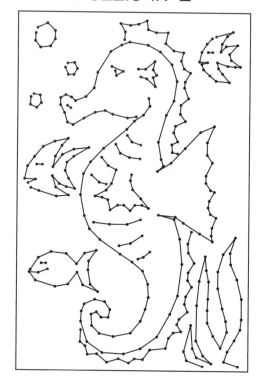

Puzzle #73

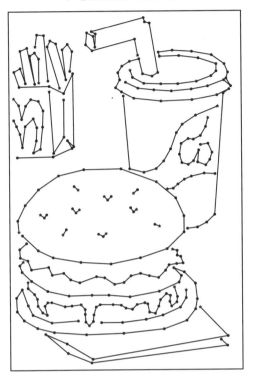

Puzzle #74

Puzzle #75

Puzzle #76

Puzzle #77

Puzzle #78

Puzzle #79

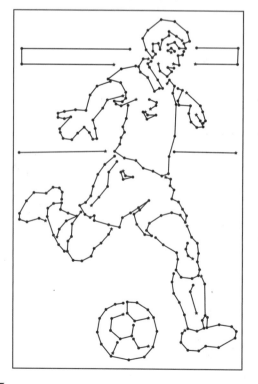

Puzzle #80